GUERRILLA MARKETING FOR SPAS

by

Jay Conrad Levinson
&
Terri Levine

ISBN-13: 978-1475224665

ISBN-10: 1475224664

All rights reserved. No part of this book may be reproduced in any form, except for the inclusion of brief quotations to review, without permission in writing from the author/publisher.

Guerrilla Marketing for Spas

Table of Contents

Foreword 1

Testimonials 2

Introduction 4

Chapter 1 - The Essence of Guerrilla Marketing 6

Chapter 2 - Paving the Way For Guerrilla Success 26

Chapter 3 - Growing Geometrically 58

Chapter 4 - Weapons for Marketing Yourself 78

Chapter 5 - Weapons for Marketing Yourself Through Others.100

Chapter 6 - Be the Expert 134

Chapter 7 - Leveraging Your Marketing Efforts 144

Chapter 8 - Planning Your Attack 152

Conclusion 159

The 200 Weapons of Guerrilla Marketing..........................161

Foreword

What you will find in this book is unlike the norm. Terri Levine has found a way to simplify a complex process so that you can absolutely manage, define and control your outcomes. Nothing about this book is based on theory. I know firsthand that Terri has based these concepts on her own experience and the experience of her clients, and she has proven that these strategies work.

She has broken down the most important Guerrilla marketing concepts into consumable pieces, making them achievable. Marketing may have been overwhelming and confusing to you before, but with these precise and effective nuggets, you'll no longer need to spend time whacking your head against a wall. Terri shows you how to work smart and maximize every effort you put out. This will be the

Guerrilla Marketing for Spas

most important book you will read this year to increase the success of your Spa.

Joel Bauer

Speaker, Trainer, Wealth Mentor

Testimonials

"Guerrilla Marketing for Spas is a powerful and targeted "must read" for any spa owner. The ideas and information are insightful and provide a unique step by step formula, sprinkled with refreshing concepts that are easy to implement. This book will inspire and guide you while it motivated and enables you to be the best. It will change you and your business."

Marianne Torhus - www.bailineusa.com

"From the moment I opened the book I was engulfed in the endless missed opportunities I had not yet taken within our current marketing practices. I surely didn't know, what I didn't know, that thanks to Guerrilla Marketing, I know now! Guerrilla Marketing for Spas is the PERFECT book to take your salon and/or spa to the next level! We have already begun applying some of the book's best practices and are so thrilled with the immediate results and are eagerly waiting to see how grand our long term ROI (return on

Guerrilla Marketing for Spas

investment) will be from following Guerrilla Marketing's guidelines to success! Thank you Terri for sharing this amazing business tool with us, we're looking forward to our best year ever thanks to Guerrilla Marketing!"

Melissa Huetter, Owner - Indigo Salon, Spa & Boutique

"I have owned my own spa for over 16 years and I have coached and educated salon and spa owners around the country on best business practices. Through the years the lack of information and practical techniques regarding marketing for our specialized needs has burdened owners and cost companies significantly in ineffective advertising expenses. 'Guerrilla Marketing for Spas' bridges this gap and is a must-read for spa owners intending to be truly successful in the new economy!"

Roseannae Klementisz, Owner - The Body Serene Day Spa

Introduction

With an increasing number of Spas entering the market and with businesses in general closing their doors in droves these days, taking responsibility for the marketing of your Spa is more important than ever.

The problem is that most Spa owners don't specialize in marketing. If you did, you probably would have opened a marketing business, right? So, how do you know what to do? What methods are best? Which ones will work and which ones won't? Which ones are too much of a gamble and which ones are worth it? What are the best ways to spend your marketing budget?

We live in a world where we are bombarded with marketing messages in every place we go and everything we do. With all of the possible ways to market your Spa, it can certainly be overwhelming and confusing. Many business owners find themselves trapped in confusion, trying out different marketing methods, with none of them landing in success.

If you don't do it right, you risk losing a lot of money, time and effort, not to mention losing your business altogether. It is fortunate you found this book because with it comes clarity, solutions and effective plans of action. You're about to learn how to use no-cost and low-cost methods to grow your Spa to where you want it to be. You're about to learn what works and what doesn't, as well as what is most important for you, as a Spa owner, to focus on. You'll learn to think like a Guerrilla, so you can get your business in the front line and be in control of your profits and successes. Let's begin.

Chapter 1 - The Essence of Guerrilla Marketing

What is Guerrilla Marketing?

Marketing is every single correspondence any part of your business has with any part of the public. People often think of marketing as just sending out postcards or having a website, but it is so much more than that. Every impression you make and every interaction you have with the public is marketing you in one way or another.

Guerrilla marketers view marketing as a circle that begins with creative ideas for generating revenue and loops around with the intention of attaining a large number of repeat and referral customers. If your marketing is only based on gaining new sales, it is not a circle, and in that case, it is a straight line leading to bankruptcy.

Guerrilla Marketing for Spas

Fortune 500 companies spend millions on traditional marketing methods, but small businesses can't compete in those markets and they need another way. That is why Guerrilla marketing was created – to offer small businesses the opportunity to launch no-cost and inexpensive marketing weapons that are effective and produce a high return. At the essence of Guerrilla marketing are unconventional tactics that substitute time, energy and imagination for money.

The Differences Between Traditional Marketing and Guerrilla Marketing

Guerrilla Marketing is marketing that is unconventional and non-traditional. Since Spas don't generally have millions to spend on traditional marketing methods, they can refer to Guerrilla marketing tactics to get results. There are 19 factors

Guerrilla Marketing for Spas

that differentiate Guerrilla marketing from old-fashioned, traditional marketing:

1. With Guerrilla marketing, the investment is in time, energy, imagination and knowledge, instead of in money.
2. With Guerrilla marketing, the science of psychology and the laws of human nature are used, instead of guesswork.
3. With Guerrilla marketing, results are measured by profits, instead of by traffic, responses or gross sales.
4. Guerrilla marketing is geared to small businesses, instead of companies with limitless bank accounts.
5. With Guerrilla marketing, there is a fervent devotion to customer follow-up, instead of ignoring customers once they have purchased.

Guerrilla Marketing for Spas

6. With Guerrilla marketing, the mystique of the entire marketing process is removed and clarified, instead of intimidating small business owners.

7. With Guerrilla marketing, cooperation (helping others and letting them help you) is a cornerstone, instead of competing with other businesses.

8. Guerrilla marketers know that long-term relationships are paramount in the 21st century, so they are dedicated to building relationships, instead of focusing solely on making sales.

9. Guerrilla marketers know that marketing combinations are more effective than using only single marketing weapons, such as advertising.

10. Guerrilla marketing allows you to grow geometrically by increasing each transaction,

getting repeat sales and adding new customers, instead of growing linearly by only adding new customers one at a time.

11. Guerrilla marketing suggests that you should grow if you want as long as you maintain your focus, instead of growing only through diversifying.

12. Guerrilla marketers aim their marketing message at individuals, instead of at groups.

13. With Guerrilla marketing, relationships are counted up at the end of the month instead of sales, since relationships are the foundation of increased sales.

14. Guerrilla marketers are always thinking of what they can give to their customers and prospects, instead of thinking of what they can take. (In

this information age, they especially give away information.)

15. Guerrilla marketers embrace technology instead of avoiding technology, knowing that technophobia is fatal nowadays.

16. With Guerrilla marketing, all forms of marketing are intentional, even down to how the phone is answered and the attire they wear, instead of it being haphazard and unintentional.

17. Guerrilla marketing aims to gain consent from people to receive marketing materials, instead of marketing to people simply to make the sale.

18. Guerrilla marketing is a dialogue with both parties communicating interactively, instead of it being a monologue with one person doing all the communicating.

19. With Guerrilla marketing, advertising is not the only form of marketing since it arms you with 200 different marketing weapons, of which advertising is only one of them.

Because of these 19 differences between traditional marketing and Guerrilla marketing, a void has been filled in the world of marketing, which explains why Guerrilla marketing books are the most widely-read marketing books in existence. As a Spa looking to market effectively, inexpensively, and uniquely, you are in the right place.

16 Secrets of Guerrilla Marketing

By learning the following 16 Guerrilla marketing secrets, you will set yourself apart from the Spas that think marketing is nothing more than advertising. To acquire a good understanding of Guerrilla marketing,

Guerrilla Marketing for Spas

all you need to do is focus on the following 16 words, ending with the letters "ent."

1. COMMITMENT – A mediocre marketing plan that has commitment behind it will always prove more profitable than a brilliant marketing plan without commitment.

    Once you plan out your marketing strategies, stick with them. Failure often comes from "trying tactics out" for a short time and never giving them the full time they need to succeed. Most marketing methods are not automatic.

2. INVESTMENT – Marketing should be viewed as an investment, not as an expense.

    Spas that view marketing as an expense will drop their marketing budget once times get tough, causing them to lose even more opportunities to bring in business. Luckily

Guerrilla Marketing for Spas

Guerrilla marketing uses low cost and no cost weapons, so the investment is more in time and energy than in money (although some monetary investment is often necessary).

3. CONSISTENT – Restraint and repetition are great allies of the Guerrilla marketer, because in staying consistent with your marketing message, you gain the trust of your prospects. Don't expect your potential prospects to remember your Spa the first time they hear of you. Stay consistent in putting yourself out there so that, over time, they will recognize you exist and choose you as their trusted choice. If you don't stay consistent, the marketing you did do is often pointless.

4. CONFIDENT – Studies have shown that confidence is the number one reason people do

business with a company, followed by quality, service, selection, and then price.

Every aspect of your Spa should make the client or prospect feel confident in you. Most people are very protective of who they will allow to assist them with their appearance and wellbeing. No one wants to get a bad massage or be burned by over-heated rocks, so you need to portray that they can trust you, and then deliver.

5. PATIENT – Slow and steady always wins the race. Without practicing patience, it will be difficult to practice commitment and consistency, to view marketing as an investment and to make prospects confident in you. Patience is required to make Guerrilla marketing work.

You want clients to come through your doors in droves, but it can't happen without patience. No one wants to hear that slow and steady wins the race, but when you have faith in that strategy, you will keep your doors open as business increases every day, instead of closing them because you were too impatient to wait for the abundance to come.

6. ASSORTMENT – It is the rare case when a single marketing tactic works on its own. That's why Guerrillas use combinations and a wide assortment of marketing weapons to gain and regain their customers.

When you combine a wide assortment of marketing weapons with a well-devised plan of action, you win. When your arsenal is vast, the victory is greater. So, fire as many weapons at once as you can, as long as you are firing them accurately and effectively.

7. CONVENIENT – Guerrillas respect their clients' and prospects' time; therefore, they make it easy and convenient to do business with them. Your industry is one where your clients are electing to come to you fully because they "want" a service done. They aren't coming to you because they have a medical condition that needs attention. Therefore, it is even more important that you make it convenient for them to come to you. If you are open only from 9:00 – 5:00, for example, you are choosing to serve only stay-at-home moms and those who don't have typical day jobs. To open your services up to those who can't come during those hours, you

will need to make it convenient for them by opening your doors at more diverse hours.

8. SUBSEQUENT – A Guerrilla marketer knows that when they've made a sale, it is only the beginning of their marketing efforts and their relationship with that customer. They know that the real profits are in repeat and referral business.

As a Spa owner, you must view your interaction with new clients as the beginning of a relationship that is based on what you can do to help them. For example, you can base the relationship on assisting them to manage stress through creating the peace and calm they desire. Nurture them and show that you are there for them, so they will want to come back to you when they decide to have another de-stress session.

9. AMAZEMENT – Guerrilla marketers know the amazing details that make their company stand out. Instead of taking those things for granted, they make sure their marketing portrays their importance.

What is the amazement factor that will wow your prospects into looking to you for their Spa desires? If you don't know it, you need to figure it out so that your marketing from this point forward can reveal that amazement to your target clients.

10. MEASUREMENT – When you practice Guerrilla marketing, you always measure your results, noticing what weapons hit the bulls-eye and which ones missed the target.

If you don't measure it, you are throwing darts at a board that has an invisible bulls-eye, and since you never know when you hit that bulls-eye, you will have to continue wasting time and money on marketing tactics that don't work just because you don't even know which ones do work. Save yourself the trouble and measure your success so you can easily eliminate the methods that continually miss the target and focus your efforts on those that hit. This strategy alone will set your Spa apart from others.

11. INVOLVEMENT – Staying involved with your client relationships by following up with them is key to gaining repeat sales and referrals. Successful Spas know that it costs six times as much to gain new clients as it does to reenlist

satisfied clients. Therefore, they make sure to involve their clients in their marketing efforts for life.

12. **DEPENDENT** – Encourage cooperation by being dependent on others and gaining their dependence on you as well.

    Your clients depend on you to fulfill your promise to provide services that will give them the results they seek. You depend on your clients to provide you with compensation for the work you do. Nurture that dependency because without it, you have no Spa.

13. **ARMAMENT** – Technology is the armament, or the main weapon, necessary to wage battle for Guerrillas.

    There are a ton of technologies available for Spas to take advantage of. Do take advantage of them, but make sure the technology you choose is enhancing the services you provide. If you let technology drive your service offerings and don't let technology overwhelm you, you'll be armed with valuable weapons that will lead to a winning Spa.

14. CONSENT – Guerrillas know that gaining consent from their prospects to send their marketing materials creates a database of interested consumers.

    Marketing to someone who has no interest in having Spa treatments is obtrusive and when it comes to e-mail marketing, it is illegal. The most effective marketing comes from marketing to the people who raise their hand and want information. Create an army of prospects who signed up for your information. Then stay consistent and keep them involved. That's the strategy for a winning campaign.

15. CONTENT – The content a Guerrilla provides is high quality and is focused on substance, rather than style.

    To gain consent as discussed above, you will most likely be giving out some information that those potential clients are seeking. Make sure your content is quality content that is rich in value, so you ensure they will gain confidence in you and think of you when they are looking for a Spa. Shortchanging the content you put out will only turn people away.

16. AUGMENT – Guerrillas always strengthen their marketing with other weapons, no matter how successful the marketing is.

When a tactic works for you, the best thing you can do is ask yourself how you can get an even louder bang for an even smaller buck next time. How can you make your website more effective? What new weapons can you supplement your current marketing plan with to strengthen your overall campaign?

Why Spas That Use Guerrilla Marketing Tactics Will Get Ahead

As a Spa owner, you need to market outside of the box to ensure success. Your industry is one of the fastest growing industries in the United States, and the barriers to enter the market are minimal, which means competition is fierce. Because of this, many Spa owners unfortunately spend almost 40% of their revenue on marketing. That's not a good business model and it leads to strained profits in no time.

Guerrilla Marketing for Spas

Guerrilla marketing focuses on highly effective tactics that are low cost or no cost, allowing you to stop cutting into your profits while increasing them at the same time.

Guerrilla marketing means that you'll stand out from your competitors because you will be unique in your approach.

By putting into action the Guerrilla marketing techniques in this book, you will have the ability to advance your business, developing a network of prospects and clients who will keep coming back and who will refer others to you at the same time.

Chapter 2 - Paving the Way For Guerrilla Success

The 7 Sentence Guerrilla Marketing Strategy

To launch an effective marketing campaign for your Spa, you will need to follow two guidelines: (1) *Start with a plan* and (2) *commit to that plan*. These are the two most important things you should know and get serious about if you are to succeed with Guerrilla marketing.

Without a plan of action, you will have no idea where you are headed and you'll haphazardly end up "somewhere," leaving everything up to chance. By taking the lead and using the *7 Sentence Guerrilla Marketing Strategy* you'll learn in this chapter, you'll know your clear destination of purpose, the tactics that will help you stay on course, the people you are fighting for and the means to arrive in style.

Guerrilla Marketing for Spas

Without sticking to your plan, you will never see the results you are looking for. Marketing requires consistency and tenacity. Results come over a period of time. If you create a plan and then change the plan a month or two into it, you aren't allowing yourself the time needed to determine the real effectiveness of what you have put in place. Then, any marketing you did do is probably pointless.

Over the years, it has been said that people need to see your marketing 6 times in order for them to even notice you. Then that number increased to 8. Now that our lives are speeding along even more in this fast-paced information age, that number has increased to 10-12. When you stay consistent with the plan you put in place, your ideal clients will begin to recognize you and you will gain their trust.

Guerrilla Marketing for Spas

Don't throw away time and money by trying a marketing tactic a couple of times and then moving to another method for a couple of times. Marketing in that manner has no point. Stick with the plan and evaluate the results over the long haul. Only alter the plan by tweaking the strategies after you have properly measured and evaluated whether or not they are effective over an extended period of time.

By launching many weapons at once, you will understand what it is to be a Guerrilla marketer, because you will be establishing a foolproof campaign that will yield results even if a couple of methods flop. Not every tactic will work for everybody, but by covering your bases, you will still succeed. It is also important to note that not every tactic will work for everybody *the first time.* That doesn't mean that same tactic won't work if tweaked and tried again. A well-devised plan combined with a wide assortment of weapons has success on the agenda. Stay consistent. Hold the course.

Most marketing plans consist of pages and pages of information and statistics that will only end up sitting on the shelf. When you complicate a process, you stifle the process. By keeping it simple, the plan can be referred to constantly and it can easily be used and remembered throughout every marketing effort you put out. That is the goal of the *7 Sentence Guerrilla Marketing Strategy*.

By using the *7 Sentence Guerrilla Marketing Strategy,* your marketing plan will portray real life scenarios containing specific people, the problems they are having, and the solutions your Spa provides for those problems. When you begin your market planning from that perspective, you come armed with real solutions. Too often, Spas guess at whether or not their services are wanted. Instead, they should be researching their target market, analyzing the needs of that market, and delivering what the market needs. That is called setting yourself up for success.

Guerrilla marketers know their target market inside and out. They have researched what they need and want, what problems they have, what gender and age bracket they fall into, where they live, how much money they have, what they spend their money on, what they like, what they dislike, what they buy, and where they hang out. They understand them intimately, therefore, they are able to provide them with the solutions they are seeking.

Positioning, or determining the specific niche your offering is meant to fill, is highly important to a Guerrilla marketer. When you become known for

Guerrilla Marketing for Spas

providing certain results or something unique in your niche, you become the go-to company for that need. Don't fade into the background by not setting yourself apart.

Guerrillas are sure to share their marketing plan with those who work with them, such as employees, co-workers, marketing partners and suppliers. In order to have success, there must be synergy in the minds of everyone involved, so that each person knows the plan and their role within the plan.

The *7 Sentence Guerrilla Marketing Strategy* is a simple and concise outline of all of the essential components that are necessary to market your product or service. As the name implies, the entire plan is represented in seven sentences, yet it is comprehensive and effective. The components include:

Guerrilla Marketing for Spas

1. Your target market(s)
2. Your niche in your market(s)
3. The purpose of your marketing
4. The benefits you provide to your clients
5. The marketing weapons you will use
6. The identity of your business
7. Your budget

Let's walk through each component in more detail.

1 – Know Your Target Market(s)

You can't hit a marketing bulls-eye without having a target for that bulls-eye to reside on. You can't be the Spa for everyone in the world. Not everyone wants what Spas offer, and out of the people who do, not all of them want what you specifically offer. Plus, not all of them are the type of person you are able to treat best. Too often, business owners are afraid of leaving anyone out of their marketing, so they end up speaking to everyone, which really means they are speaking to no one. If you don't have a narrow target market, a specific group of people who are ideal for what you offer, then you may as well stop all marketing efforts now.

The Guerrilla marketer knows that when they get specific as far as whom they want to service, they set themselves up as the go-to Spa for that specific group of people. Instead of having the frustration and stress that comes along with being one of thousands of Spas that offer what you offer, you become one of tens that would serve as the obvious choice for specific individuals.

The beauty of catering to a target market is that as the owner of your Spa, you end up loving what you

Guerrilla Marketing for Spas

do much more because you are serving the ideal clients that you love serving, instead of having only a few ideal clients and tons of non-ideal clients that you aren't able to help as well. In addition, your marketing efforts become much easier because you now know where to market your services since you know where your ideal clients hang out. You know what they can afford and what they are willing to spend their money on, so there are no guessing games involved. You know what they like and dislike, so you can better grab their attention. And in general, instead of spending tons of time trying to catch a few good prospects in a vast sea of people, you are able to build a following of ideal clients that value you and trust you among all the rest.

The following questions will help you discover and narrow your target markets. This is where you get to begin creatively thinking like a Guerrilla. As you go through each question, set up a 2-minute drill. These work best on paper (not on a computer) and they involve setting a timer for two minutes as you write as fast as you can any and all ideas that flow into your mind. Don't judge what comes – just jot it all down, because you'll be surprised how a "crazy" idea can spark a "more sane" one down the line. This process allows you to get a lot of creative ideas down quickly and effectively without laboring over it or over-thinking each question. Don't hold yourself up – just get right into it.

Here are the powerful questions to help you discover your target market(s). Go ahead and do a 2-minute drill for each question:

1. What are all the possible types of clients that can benefit from your services?

2. What kinds of clients do you love to treat?
3. What kinds of clients are the most lucrative?
4. What kinds of clients are you great at treating?
5. What causes people to become Spa clients?

When complete, go back and notice if there are any themes showing up. Highlight the answers that you are most drawn to. Then analyze which markets would be most profitable for you, which ones are easiest to find and which ones you would enjoy working with the most. Cross off any markets that you wouldn't enjoy working with or that you aren't qualified to assist. These additional 2-minute drills can help you:

1. Do clients in this market tend to seek out Spas? If not, remove them right away. You want people who willingly want what you offer, not people that you have to convince.

2. Do clients in this category have the money to invest for Spa services? There is no reason to spend your time marketing to people who can't even afford your services.

3. Are clients in this category the decision makers? If not, don't waste your time and money marketing to them.

4. Is this market segment clearly defined and specific? For example, "Women" would not be specific, but "Women in Their 30's and 40's looking to renew their energy and lose weight" is.

5. Are there enough clients in this category to build your business from? Though your market needs to be narrow, you still need enough people wanting the service you are offering to make it a success.

Guerrilla Marketing for Spas

6. Is this a group of people that would be easy enough to reach? Are there organizations, associations, publications, mailing lists, Internet forums, etc. for this market segment?

7. Are you credible or can you quickly become credible in this segment? Can you borrow someone else's credibility that can help introduce you to that market segment?

Once you have a list of possible markets, narrow it down further to start with just one. You can always add more markets later, but if you try to market to more than one at a time, you will fall back into the issue you are trying to get away from – marketing to everyone, and therefore, no one.

2 – Know Your Niche in That Market

Your niche is the service you specialize in offering to your target market. This should be pretty

Guerrilla Marketing for Spas

simple, but make sure you are clear on your specialties in your industry. All Spas, for example, might offer dietary advice and personal trainers for health and fitness, but not *all* Spas specialize in *all* of those services and may focus more on rest and relaxation.

Take some time to determine what you stand for.

Here are some additional powerful questions for your 2-minute drills that can help you discover your niche:

1. What is your position in your marketplace?
2. What services are you great at?
3. What do you do better than others in the industry?
4. What service do you have a particular amount of experience in?

3 – Know the Purpose of Your Marketing

Knowing the purpose of your marketing pertains to knowing exactly what step you want your clients to take as a result of your marketing. For example, do you want them to come out and visit your Spa, clip and use a coupon, sign up for your free e-book on your website, purchase a weekend package, come to your live seminar, complete a survey, ask for more information, come in for a tour of your Spa, etc?

Knowing the purpose of your marketing allows you to have a clear call-to-action in all of your marketing efforts. Unless someone is actively seeking a Spa at this particular moment, they are not going to call you on their own. Marketing is all about timing, and unless someone is ready for your services right now, they aren't going to be looking for you. That is why you need to capture their interest and then tell them what you want them to do next. If, for example, you find someone who might be inclined to have an interest in the services you provide down the line, and you get them to sign up for your free e-book on your website now, then you have the opportunity to keep in front of them and be the Spa they choose when the time is right. Be proactive and call them to action now.

When you know the purpose of your marketing, your marketing efforts will be easier, because when you have clearly defined what you want, it becomes easier for you to know how to get what you want. If, for example, you really want to grow the skin care segment of your business, then you know that you don't need to market to people in their twenties and you know how to grab your ideal clients' attention.

Guerrilla Marketing for Spas

You know that offering your prospective clients a free seminar on skin health would probably bring in a lot of interested people. It allows you to analyze every marketing move you make based on your purpose.

4 – Know the Benefits You Provide to Your Clients

The benefits you provide are your competitive advantages. It is the awesomeness of your unique company that sets you apart and intrigues people. It is what makes you the number one choice in the eyes of your ideal clients.

Plenty of other business owners are offering the exact same services that you provide in your Spa. So why should someone hire you? Discovering the answer to that question is the key to your success.

Until you know what makes you the clear choice in the Spa industry, you will not be able to clearly convey to others why they should choose you. If *you* don't know why they should choose you, how can you expect them to know?

When you are developing this part of your plan, make sure you are determining the *benefits* you provide, not the *features*. A benefit is a solution to a problem. A feature is a factual statement about a product or service being promoted.

For example, if you offer a skin health program for women, a benefit could be that they would regain their youthful complexion. A feature would be the high tech methods you use to achieve that complexion.

An easy way to get to the benefits you provide is to ask yourself, "What do your clients really buy when they invest in your Spa services?" Are they buying confidence? Are they buying beauty? Youth? Convenience?

What is the pain they are experiencing? What is the solution to that pain that you provide? When you can offer clients a solution to their problem, then you no longer need to even consider hard sells or trying to convince anyone that you have what they need. They will convince themselves.

Determining the benefits or solutions you provide your clients with will give you power in your marketing. Every tactic you choose will represent the benefits you offer, and that means that your marketing efforts will be aligned, clear, and most of all, attention-grabbing.

5 – Know the Marketing Weapons You Will Use

Your marketing plan should include a wide assortment of weapons you will launch to market your Spa. Remember, when you combine weapons together, that is where the strength of your marketing plan lies. Instead of having all of your eggs in one basket, disperse them about so that the weapons that end up being more effective can outweigh those that are weak.

Choose your tactics from the list in the back of the book and stick with them as you measure your results. A more detailed explanation of several of the most powerful weapons for Spas will be explained in the pages to come, as well.

6 – Know the Identity of Your Business

You've already determined the benefits you provide to your clients. Now it is time to establish how those benefits can shine and manifest themselves into the identity of your Spa. Your identity is extremely important because it is the impression your business will leave on others. It is how you will be recognized and remembered. It is what will make you stand out from your competitors.

How do you want to be perceived? What are the values and strengths that you want to be known for? This is where you let your awesomeness shine. This is what will make people remember you when they think of visiting a Spa.

Examples can be in areas of outstanding customer service, competency, ethics, quality, price, experience, or anything else that you want to be known for.

7 – Know Your Budget

It is important to know ahead of time how much money you will devote to marketing so you can plan for it and be consistent with it. When a budget is in place, you know what you have to work with each month, so you can plan your marketing tactics accordingly. You can also feel good about the marketing dollars you spend, because since you have determined how much you will put back into your business for marketing, it becomes an investment, instead of an expense.

For the sake of this marketing plan, your budget will be expressed in a percentage of your projected gross sales. In other words, it is the percentage that you are putting back into the business to go toward marketing. Depending on where you are in your business, a good marketing budget is usually between 10-20% of your revenue. Much more than that will leave your profit margin too narrow, and less than that will not allow you to bring in enough profits to create and maintain a successful business.

An example of a completed *7 Sentence Guerrilla Marketing Strategy* could be:

> Renew Spa serves local business people in their 30's, 40's and 50's who want to renew their energy and fitness, for which we will position ourselves as the leader in health and fitness services. The purpose of our marketing is to acquire sign ups to our newsletter in order to stay in touch with those opted-in people who will come to us when they are ready to boldly

claim the healthy fitness that is within them by finding the right Spa. This will be accomplished by establishing our superior knowledge and experience in the health and wellness fields, making us the number one trusted resource for safe and quality treatments in the Northeast Philadelphia area. The weapons we will use to convey this marketing message are postcards, classified ads, free give-aways, outside signs, indoor signs, direct mail, list building, website, landing page, auto responders, blogs, e-books, webinars, joint ventures, pay per click ads, case studies, networking, call-to-actions, gift certificates, positioning and copywriting ability. In all of our marketing, we will convey our unique ability to inspire health and wellness to the outside by the high quality talent and skill of our qualified staff, as well as the cheerful and fun atmosphere we create and maintain for our clientele. 20% of sales will be allocated to marketing.

Creating Your Unique Core Positioning Statement

When someone asks you what you do, if you say, "I own a Spa," you're not going to gain much interest. Some people might say, "Oh, that's nice," and ask you where your Spa is, but the conversation isn't going to go much further.

People rarely respond to the "What do you do?" question in a way that actually entices the other person to want to know more. Although asking someone what you do seems to be a question about you, your answer should actually be the opposite. That's because people are not really interested in what you do. They become intrigued, however, when you explain how you can help *them*. Remember, when people ask you, "What do you do?" they are really asking, "How can you help me?" Your answer should explain the benefits you offer others through the work you do.

It is also important to respond to the "What do you do?" question in a single, concise sentence. Nobody wants to try to make small talk and end up feeling trapped by a one-sided conversation with a person going on and on about what they do. Don't hog the conversation. Remember, the way to win people over is by talking less and listening more. Give them the benefits you offer in one sentence and then shut up. If they respond, you continue on with another simple follow up statement. They will show you if they want you to say more by their interest level and the questions they ask (or don't ask).

The one-sentence message you want to craft is called your *Core Unique Positioning Statement* (CUPS). Since you have already come up with the benefits you provide to your Spa clients in the fourth sentence of your *7 Sentence Guerrilla Marketing Strategy*, creating your CUPS should be a piece of cake.

When you can state the solution you provide to your clients' problems in a concise, intriguing statement, it will become clear to them whether you are a fit for them or not. You won't need to ramble on and on trying to explain what you do, giving them credentials and fancy terms they won't understand or even care about anyway. You'll pique their interest, or you won't. And if you don't, it's okay because it just

Guerrilla Marketing for Spas

means they don't need the solutions you provide, but someone else will.

Your *Core Unique Positioning Statement* is simply stating the most critical problems your clients want solved and the goals they would give anything to achieve. To determine those things, you must ask your clients. You can't expect to guess what their biggest problems are and get it right. Survey your ideal clients so you can get to the heart of their real issues and start getting people excited to come to your Spa. You can survey them by simply calling or e-mailing them, or you can use survey software offered through sites like www.surveymonkey.com, www.googledocssurveytool.com or www.zoomerang.com. All you need to ask is: "If I could help you with one beauty issue in the next three to six months, but only one, what issue would that

Guerrilla Marketing for Spas

be?" If you don't have a base of clients at this point because you are just starting out, you can find a website where your ideal prospects hang out, and ask them your survey question in exchange for a gift, such as an e-book or special report.

Once you have captured the answers, the frequent theme or recurring answer will become your CUPS. The outcome the client will get from coming to your Spa is what your CUPS should state. An example of a good CUPS is:

"I restore youth and confidence in women who are in the prime of their life."

You will notice that in that statement, you are informed of what that Spa owner essentially does and whom they do it for, but they never mentioned that they have a Spa.

Guerrilla Marketing for Spas

The formula for creating a good CUPS is as follows:

1. Action word – Notice that the above example begins with an action word instead of a description word, like stylist or esthetician. The action word should clearly show how you help your clients.
2. Your solution – This is where you explain the benefit you provide, which is the solution to the problem your ideal clients have.

Without a *Core Unique Positioning Statement*, you will have to make hard sells, trying to convince people you have what they need. You will also have a very hard time building a successful Spa or following the strategies in the rest of this book. This is the foundation from which the rest of your marketing efforts will follow. Every time you are asked, "What do

Guerrilla Marketing for Spas

you do?" you now have an answer that is intriguing and clearly states how you can help others.

Creating Your Follow Up Statement

Now that you have your *Core Unique Positioning Statement*, you will need to have a follow-up statement prepared, because you are going to generate so much interest that people are going to ask you to tell them more.

When they show interest and ask for more, you follow up by saying that you own a Spa and then describing another benefit statement that explains how you get the results you promised in your CUPS. This should also be one simple, concise sentence. An example could be:

"I provide Spa treatments such as massages, relaxation remedies, skin care, and fitness programs,

Guerrilla Marketing for Spas

allowing me to renew confidence and bring out the inner beauty in women over 40."

Armed with your *Core Unique Positioning Statement* and your follow up statement, you will be able to walk into any networking or sales situation with confidence. You will be able to be yourself and not worry about "selling." And you now have a clear message to carry through to all of your marketing materials and communications. Plus you will set yourself worlds apart from the numerous Spa owners who answer, "I own a Spa" to the question, "What do you do?"

Chapter 3 - Growing Geometrically

Guerrilla marketers work smart. They are creative in their thinking. They practice leveraging techniques to get the most out of every marketing weapon they launch. They don't just try to grow in a linear fashion by adding new clients. Instead, they focus on growing geometrically.

Geometric growth takes place when you not only add new clients, but you also add additional dimensions through repeat business, through enlarging each transaction and through gaining referrals from your existing clients.

It costs six times as much in marketing dollars to sell your services to a new client as it does to sell your services to existing clients. As you can see, the more you market geometrically, the less money you invest in marketing.

Getting Repeat Sales With a Keep-in-Touch Program

If you want your Spa to succeed, then you will practice follow-up the way a Guerrilla marketer does. The number one reason Spas lose clients after an initial treatment is because they ignore their clients. 68% of all business lost in America is due to apathy after the sale. Don't contribute to that statistic.

Guerrilla marketers know that marketing doesn't end once the sale is over. To them, the end of the initial service is only the beginning of the relationship. They keep in touch with their clients from that point forward in a manner that nurtures and further develops that relationship. They are able to transform their list of previous clients into a tribe of repeat clients who genuinely enjoy paying for the services they buy, and who tout the relationship they have with their Spa to their friends and family.

You learned that it costs six times as much in marketing dollars to sell your services to a new client as it does to sell your services to existing clients. That is why follow-up is paramount for Guerrilla marketers. It makes the most sense to base the bulk of your marketing efforts on follow-up because it is a great asset that creates a huge return on investment for years and years to come.

Develop your keep-in-touch programs for your Spa and follow them. You will see the results over time. Your programs might include e-mail blasts, personal e-mails, snail mail letters, postcards, phone

Guerrilla Marketing for Spas

calls, personal visits, gift packages, greeting cards and anything else you can creatively think of. Here is an example of an effective keep-in-touch program:

> Send your clients a thank you note within 48 hours of their first service.
>
> Then make a phone call or send a letter 30 days later to make sure everything went well with their treatment after they left your office and to see if they have any questions. What this does is to help solidify the relationship you started when you treated them. They come to understand that they are not just a number to you. They sense they are important to you, and they feel the relationship beginning.

Another form of follow-up should come within 90 days to inform them of a new or related service you provide. It could even be a product or service offered from one of your fusion marketing partners.

Within six months, your client should hear from you again with something such as an upcoming promotion that would benefit the client.

In nine months, send them a letter asking for the names of three people who could benefit from being on your mailing list.

Be sure to send them a card to celebrate the one-year anniversary of their first service, with a coupon or gift certificate for another service.

In fifteen months after the first service, send them a questionnaire asking questions that will help you understand your client better. Be up front and explain to them in the accompanying letter that you value their time so you have chosen to ask them only questions that will help you understand them better in order to provide them with more valuable service and treatments.

After eighteen months, send an announcement about more products and/or services that tie in with the original purchase they had made.

Throughout this process, you also want to be feeding useful and relevant information to your clients in the form of a newsletter or e-mail blast. It could contain articles you have written or that you have compiled from others. It can be easily done using an auto responder, which allows you to set up e-mails on a set schedule that will automatically get sent out without you having to do anything once you have set up the timeline. The importance of this keep-in-touch method is that it keeps you in front of your clients in a way that is not sales-like and that sets you up as the go-to professional for the services you provide. They will gain respect and appreciation for the helpful information you send their way, and they will appreciate it even more because it is not presented in a hard-sell manner. If they need the service or product you are sending them information about, they will seek you out – you don't need to constantly be selling to them for them to understand they can come to you for that product or service.

This newsletter process is also effective when following up with *prospective* clients that you can't send other follow up methods to, like thank you cards and referral requests. With this method, you're still able to keep in front of them and establish yourself as the go-to Spa when they are ready for a treatment.

By marketing like a Guerrilla and using keep-in-touch tactics, you will change the lifetime value of each client considerably. Let's say your average service yields $50 in revenue for your Spa. If you don't keep in touch, it is very likely that $50 will end up being the lifetime value of that client. But if you put a keep-in-touch program in place as suggested above, you will most likely increase the purchases from that client from one to six or more, plus they will often have referred additional clients your way. The relationship you have created with this client becomes a bond that can last 20 years with additional purchases being made and additional referrals coming your way year after year. Due to your follow up, the lifetime value of that client can easily change from $50 to $50,000 and beyond. Imagine what can happen when you follow-up with *all* of your clients. Plus, don't forget, you've done all of that with a very low-cost marketing investment.

Developing a Referral-Based Business

Referrals generally cost nothing to obtain, but they are often the best form of marketing because the person being referred was given a testimonial from a third party that they trust, so they come to you already believing you can give them what they are looking for. Think about your own situation. If you complain to a friend about back pain and they end up raving to you about their chiropractor and how much he has helped them and how important he is to their wellbeing, do you think you will give that chiropractor a call? When you do call, do you think you are going to need to be convinced that he is the right chiropractor for you, or do you think you will go in there already sure he is? That is why referrals are so powerful.

To begin getting referrals, always ask where a new client was referred from and then let them know that referrals are an important part of your business. This sets them up from the beginning understanding how much you value referrals and inspires them to want to help out when you do ask them for referrals.

Write to your customers at least twice a year asking for the names of people who could benefit from being added to your mailing list. Ask for the names of three people (this keeps it a small enough number that it is easy for them to provide) and include a postage paid envelope to make it as easy as possible for them. You could even explain that you will be giving the people they refer a special gift that they will value and that they, themselves, will also receive the gift.

Whether you asked for the referral or not, be sure to give thank you gifts to those who refer new clients to you. It expresses your gratitude for their kind act and demonstrates that you appreciate them going out of their way for you. It helps to further

Guerrilla Marketing for Spas

develop the relationship and makes it that much more likely that they will continue to refer clients to you.

Enlarging Each Transaction With Packaging

Another effective way to grow geometrically is to increase the size of each transaction. This is done best through packaging. When offering massage services, for example, offer package deals that allow the client to save money if they purchase 5 massage sessions at once redeemable for the next 3 months.

Another way to create packages is to combine complementary treatments that work well together into a package and offer it at a discount.

By offering packages, the customer gets more value because you offer the package at a discount from what they would pay for each component separately. Plus, you also benefit because this method entices a higher purchase from the client so you increase your average sale. When you do that for each client, you increase your revenue considerably.

The key is to make sure the additional components in the package not only complement each other, but that they also add tons of value for the client. A Guerrilla marketer never tries to get extra money out of a client just to get extra money. It must happen only because you know that the added products and services will benefit them and add tremendous value for them. If you design your packages right, your clients will line up to purchase them and they will thank you for providing them.

You can also include additional components in the package that don't really cost you anything but

Guerrilla Marketing for Spas

that add even more value, such as your e-book or a subscription to your newsletter.

As a Guerrilla marketer, always be asking yourself how you can continually add value for your clients without a large investment on your part.

Reactivating Inactive Clients

You've learned how to create a keep-in-touch program to use for all new clients you receive from this point forward, but how should you begin re-engaging clients who have been inactive for some time now? You can start with writing them a reactivation letter.

In the letter, you remind them of the results they received from your treatment. Then you can mention any positive changes and/or new services you might offer, as well as explaining to them that you now offer a new way for them to get valuable information that will help them with the area they came to you for help with previously. Let them know you will be giving them a subscription to your newsletter so they can gain the value of that information. This way, you can get them right into the follow-up system you have created. A sample of the letter could look like this:

Reactivation Letter Sample:

Date

Client's name, title
Company name
Address

Dear Mr./Ms. Client,

I'm writing to thank you for coming to see us in the past. I've realized we haven't seen you in quite some time.

As you know, I helped you (INSERT THE PROBLEM YOU SOLVED FOR THEM). We were able to get beautiful results.

I've enjoyed working with you personally. So, naturally, I'm a bit surprised I haven't heard from you in quite some time. If we've done anything that might have caused you to discontinue doing business with us, I'd really appreciate it if you'd let me know. And I promise I'll do everything in my power to make it up to you. Just call my office and speak with my office manager, Jane Taylor, at (555) 555-5555 and I'll make sure your call gets through to me personally.

Also, since it's been a while since we last talked, you might not be aware that I've added a dozen new issues of my newsletter to my subscription-based archives on my website. I'd like to give you a one-year subscription to the archives with my compliments. Your personal access code that you can begin using right away is Name=Client, Password=Thanks. I hope you enjoy the health and wellness tips you'll find in the archives.

As I said, I truly regret if we caused you any inconvenience. We really value your business and I'd like to keep you a satisfied client for many years to come. In fact, I have a new treatment that is fast and effective to help you (INSERT RELATED ISSUE TO THE ONE YOU SOLVED FOR THEM) for years to come.

Thanks again for doing business with us. I'll look forward to hearing from you soon and giving you all the details on this exciting new treatment.

Sincerely,

Your Name
Your Company

Adding New Customers With a Call-to-Action

Although Guerrillas grow geometrically, instead of the normal linear method of just searching for new clients, it is still important to focus part of your marketing on gaining new clients. To do this, make sure to always use a call-to-action in every one of your marketing tactics.

How often do you see an advertisement that is nothing more than a business card printed in advertisement form? That is certainly not effective marketing and it is certainly not Guerrilla marketing. A business card size ad does not need to mimic a business card. Think outside of the box and use that 3.5" x 2" space to compel your prospective clients to do what you would like them to do. That is what a call-to-action is – it gets your audience to act, and it gets them to act in the way that *you* want them to

Guerrilla Marketing for Spas

act. Your call-to-action can come from the purpose that you wrote in number three of your *7 Sentence Guerrilla Marketing Strategy*.

A call-to-action is not a form of bribery or deception. It does not mean that you are being pushy or making people do things against their will. Believe it or not, when most people see your marketing pieces, they are not going to know what move to make unless you tell them. They might be interested in what you offer and tear out the ad or bookmark your webpage, but after that, it is so easy for you to be long forgotten in their minds. Think about it – how often do you see an interesting marketing piece and then put it aside with the greatest intentions, only to completely forget about it the next day? Life is busy and demanding. If you don't give them a reason to act, and to act *now*, you will most likely lose them. If you want your marketing to be effective, have a strong call-to-action on every marketing weapon you put out.

Some examples of strong calls-to-actions are:

- "Bring back your youth and energy TODAY and feel confident in yourself again. Get it back now by signing up for this FREE 'Renew You' seminar. Space is limited. Sign up today at www.RenewSpa.com."
- "If you've heard your wife complain one too many times about how unhappy she is with her sagging energy, give her the gift that will boost how young she feels. Energy boosting holiday packages are available now for a short time only. Don't delay. Call 222-234-5678 to order."

Chapter 4 - Weapons for Marketing Yourself

You need to market yourself, because if you don't tell the world what you offer, not many people will know about your Spa. Word of mouth is great, but it doesn't cut it in this economy. To begin with, you need to change the perception society has planted in your mind about sales practices. Guerrilla marketers don't apologize for offering their services and products to people because they know that their services and products help people. If what you offer doesn't solve a problem for people then there is no way you will sell it. It is a great thing to be able to help solve someone's problem, and to not offer a solution to someone who can use it would be criminal. If your friend was suffering from a disease and you had the medicine that would cure it, would you be afraid to offer it to them? Of course not. It is the same thing with marketing your services. Be proud of the Spa you have created and all the people you are able to help.

Here are some marketing weapons that can help you get the word out:

Lead Generation Letter

A lead generation letter is a direct mail tactic that works. If written well, it can serve to compel the recipients to take action. Do some research to compile a database that will receive the information you send by assembling together prospective clients who would have an interest in what you offer.

Armed with a database that wants what you provide, you'll meet success when you write a letter that will speak to their personal desires. Explain that you understand the problem they have, which could be low energy, weight problems, high stress levels, or any other number of health and wellness issues. Then go on describing how you can help them solve those problems. Finally, give them a call-to-action, stating that they can go to your website to download your free report (or some form of information that can help them).

This letter is not a hard sell letter because it is not asking them to buy anything. You are only explaining that you understand what they are going through and that you can help by giving them free information. For that reason, this type of letter gets a much higher response rate than a lot of direct mail.

Guerrilla Marketing for Spas

We consistently see results of a 5% response rate, whereas the typical response rate for direct mail is 1% - 2%.

Business Card

Business cards are often not effective because most people view them as just a means to hand out their contact information. In those cases, business cards are a waste of money. The way to make them effective is to use them to convey your marketing message – to transform them into a tool that markets your business, instead of just supplying contact information. If someone is not compelled to contact you, they aren't going to contact you; therefore, the business card gets thrown in the trash.

Guerrilla Marketing for Spas

Use the back of your business card to add that extra punch. It's a great place to include a couple of short testimonials and a shortened version of your *Core Unique Positioning Statement*. By doing that, you clearly and concisely explain the benefits your work provides and you demonstrate that people have gotten those results. *That* is a powerful handout.

Another idea for the back of the business card is to add a call-to-action by offering them your free report that they can sign up for on your website. The power in this method is that you pique their interest, you get them to your site where they are free to browse your offerings, and most importantly, you capture their contact information in your database, so they can be part of your keep-in-touch program.

As a Guerrilla marketer, you need to be thinking creatively with *every* marketing piece and form of communication you put out. Never make the mistake of thinking, "Well it's just a business card." Everything your prospective clients and existing clients view from you is an opportunity to win and re-win them over. Be creative.

Online Marketing

The Internet is one of the best tools available to us nowadays as Guerrilla marketers. It has never been so easy to get the word out to so many people so inexpensively. Plus, it is like having a location that never closes and is viewable by the entire world.

With the millions of people online, Guerrilla marketers remember to approach each individual personally when marketing online. Your web copy should be written as if you are speaking to that individual person alone. It should feel like an intimate conversation where you answer the questions they are asking in their head, you show them that you understand their situation, and you provide solutions for their personal needs.

The goal people generally have when they go online is to collect information. Students no longer need encyclopedias, adults no longer need to stay up for the 11:00pm news to watch the weather for the next day, and phone books are pretty much considered dinosaurs these days. The Internet is really the world of information at your fingertips. This is important to understand so you can participate in online marketing in a way that both capitalizes on that fact and that makes your marketing campaigns easier.

A Guerrilla marketer has a website that provides the kind of information their potential clients would be searching for. A website is not an invitation to brag about how great you are, and to go on and on talking about yourself. Instead, it should be a portal of information that helps people find solutions to their problems. This is the information age, and it is powered by the Internet.

Keep websites simple, clean and easy to navigate. You have probably seen websites that are jam packed with too many words and links. It makes it a confusing and overwhelming experience, one that usually results in the viewer quickly leaving the site. Let your site walk the viewer through the questions they have in their head when they come to your site. They are probably looking to know how you have helped other individuals just like them, the results those individuals had, the additional services you offer, the reasons they should trust you and what

Guerrilla Marketing for Spas

makes you unique in relation to all the other Spa choices they have available to them. They might also be looking for articles and information on various health treatments – just remember not to present information like that in an overwhelming way. Organize your articles and blogs neatly and make it easy to navigate.

The Internet is also a place for connection to take place. In Guerrilla marketing, the focus is on building relationships, not on getting quick, one-time sales. The Internet is the perfect tool for creating that connection. With social media sites like LinkedIn, Facebook and Twitter, it is so easy to create a tribe of followers who you can offer useful and valuable information to on a regular basis. It is now easy to set yourself up as an expert so you become the go-to Spa to turn to. Social media is the perfect platform to present yourself as a caring professional who is willing to share knowledge with the goal of helping others overcome their issues. What social media is not is a place to hit people with constant advertisements. Sales will come as a result of your connection and community-attitude on social media, not from you selling your services.

E-mail Marketing

Marketing yourself via e-mail is one of the most common ways of advertising these days, and it is particularly popular with Guerrillas because it allows them to deliver their message instantly to anyone in the world for no cost. With so many people using the same tactic, it is important to set yourself apart and

Guerrilla Marketing for Spas

use Guerrilla marketing creativity to make a lasting impact.

Online newsletters are an important part of marketing in this information age, but how are you using this tactic? If you are constantly hitting your database with e-mail ads about your services, most people will just hit delete and/or they will unsubscribe from your list. Remember, it's all about the viewer and what they want. Forget about what you want. What do they want when they open an e-mail from your Spa? If you don't know, survey them to find out. Are they looking for coupons? Do they want to learn about the benefits of a new health regime? Do they want to know what they can do at home to help them maintain their health and enhance what you offer in your Spa? Do they want to learn about others who have had similar issues as them and found lasting results through a specific treatment?

Frequency is important to consider in e-mail marketing. If you are polling your database to find out what they want in e-mails from you, be sure to also ask them how frequently they want to hear from you. Everyone is different, but on average once a month for an e-mail newsletter works well because it keeps you in front of your audience without being too intrusive. Once a month is also enough when you are using other Guerrilla marketing weapons along with your e-mail marketing, because you are staying in touch in many other ways in addition to the newsletter, so they all reinforce each other.

Advertisements

Advertisements are a very large category covering many different media sources. For the sake of this section of the book, we are referring to classified ads, online classified ads, pay-per-click ads, magazine ads, newspaper ads, free ads, and ads in other people's e-zines.

More marketing funds are invested in advertising than in any other marketing weapon. It is also the way that most marketing dollars are wasted, so it is important to learn what is effective and what is not.

Guerrillas make sure all of the following 10 requirements are within each advertisement they put out. Your ads should be:

Guerrilla Marketing for Spas

1. Readable
2. Informative
3. Clear
4. Honest
5. Simple
6. On Strategy
7. Motivating
8. Competitive
9. Specific
10. Believable

When designing your ad, the most important component is the headline. Since it is so important, we have devoted a separate section to headlines, and you will learn about that in the next section.

For your overall advertisement, be sure it is interesting, it attracts attention (the right kind of attention) and it speaks to a yearning, a desire, a need or a problem the viewer has. An ad should never look like a typical business card, displaying just the name of your company and contact information. How many times have you viewed ads like that and just glanced past them because you didn't even understand what the business offered and it didn't speak to you in any way? Be creative and think outside of the box.

Take some time and review other companies' ads. Notice which ones jump out at you, which ones you are drawn to, and which ones pique your interest. Notice what they are doing and why their ads are more effective.

When using graphics in your ads, make sure the graphic adds to the idea you are presenting. Make sure it attracts attention, but isn't overpowering to the message of the ad. Make sure it is a quality image with high resolution – respect is lost immediately when low quality photos are used on marketing pieces. The art you use in your ads should be purposeful, visually stimulating, and complementary to your message.

Here is an example of an effective ad:

Free Report

High Level Energy Boost Now.

Tired of being tired, run down and no energy? Sick of supplements that don't work? Our FREE report gives you 10 easy and fast ways to restore your natural energy levels immediately. Sign up today for your FREE copy at www.XYZHEALTHSPA.com

Headlines

Headlines are by far the most important part of your marketing. Therefore, Guerrilla marketers devote the time and creativity necessary to make their headlines stellar. This is because the headline is the first impression you will make on your viewers. It's the 2-5 seconds when your viewers decide to stay with you or move on.

In an advertisement or a direct mail letter, the headline is the top line of text and is usually bold or made to stand out in some way. In a sales call, the headline is the first thing you say to your prospects. In an e-mail, it is your subject line. On a website, it is the first thing the viewer sees. In a commercial, it is the first thing that is said or shown on the screen.

Guerrilla Marketing for Spas

The importance of headlines is this: If your headline is a loser, you have three strikes against you when you step up to the plate. That pretty much says it all.

Here are 20 keys to making sure your headline is a winner (not every key applies to every headline):

1. Your headline must convey an idea or intrigue the viewer to want to learn more.
2. You must speak directly to the viewer as an individual, not as a group of people.
3. You should write your headline in news-like style.
4. Use words that create the feeling of an important announcement.
5. Test headlines that start with the word "announcing."
6. Test headlines that start with the word "new."

Guerrilla Marketing for Spas

7. Put a date in your headline if relevant.
8. If you are proud of your price, feature it in your headline.
9. Feature your easy payment plan if relevant.
10. Announce a free offer and use the word "free."
11. Offer information of value right in your headline.
12. Since Guerrillas know that marketing is really truth made fascinating, start to tell a fascinating story in your headline.
13. Begin your headline with the words "How to" when applicable.
14. Begin your headline with "why," "which," "you," "this" or "advice" when it works.
15. Use testimonial-style headlines.
16. Offer the reader a test.
17. Use a huge one-word headline.
18. Warn the reader not to delay buying.

19. Address your headline to a specific type of person.
20. Set your headline in the largest type on the page and let the headline begin your verbal presentation.

Remember that headlines should serve to get the viewer to stop on your ad. If they don't stop on your ad, they will stop on someone else's. It's your first impression and your initial bond with the viewer, so make it a good one.

The New Power of Advertising

With the birth of the Internet, advertising has been transformed forever. In years before the Internet, the focus of advertising was on making the sale. Now, however, the focus is usually on directing people to a website, where they can then access much more information than they could from an advertisement.

Marketing is now all about inspiring interactivity and gaining permission to receive further marketing messages by directing people to websites, offering free brochures and e-books, or getting them to sign up for teleseminars, for example. Once interested people have granted permission by requesting more information, that is when serious Guerrilla marketing attempts to close the sale.

To make permission-based marketing work, Guerrillas create easy-to-take actions, instead of asking them to open their wallets and spend their hard-earned money right off the bat. This type of marketing is easier for Guerrillas, because they don't have to worry about hard sells or talking anyone into buying.

Guerrilla marketers know that when they combine offline marketing with online marketing, they will see dramatic results. With the number of businesses online, you can't expect your website to be seen that easily when someone searches a keyword, such as "massage" or "fitness." Smart Guerrilla marketers promote their Spas offline in an effort to direct people to their website.

Chapter 5 - Weapons for Marketing Yourself Through Others

While you should never be ashamed to market yourself, the most powerful way to market your Spa is through others. This is because the viewers' trust level goes up considerably when they are introduced to a Spa through a third-party endorsement, rather than hearing it from a Spa tooting their own horn.

Since much of Guerrilla marketing is about forming partnerships and alliances, and working together instead of in competition, this chapter is focused on providing you with marketing weapons to help you do just that. These tactics have the power to truly transform your Spa and its profits if you practice what you read here.

Endorsement Letters

This tactic plays off of the lead generation letter strategy you learned about in the previous chapter, but with more power packed in the punch. Again, the added power comes from the third-party endorsement. While lead generation letters have been proven to yield a 5% response rate, endorsement letters bring that rate up to 10-16%. That is an incredible rate of response, so you don't want to miss this method.

It all comes down to credibility. People want to turn to a Spa they can trust. They want to be sure the treatment is going to be done properly and that they won't have any unforeseen issues to deal with after the fact. They don't want to regret their decision to have the service done. In order to get that kind of trust in a Spa, they need to know it is credible. If you just go around telling people you are credible, no one is going to believe you, because credibility is earned. How is it earned? By credible people speaking positively about the experience they had with your Spa.

You can create that credibility with an endorsement letter, which is nothing more than a letter sent out by a service provider, organization or association, printed on their stationary, endorsing you and your Spa. The letter simply talks about the success this person had with your services. They share the results they get from being your client. Then they state that they arranged for their clients, colleagues or members to receive a free report or a gift certificate for treatment or for a free evaluation from you.

The endorser is happy to send this type of letter because it allows them to offer a free gift to their clients. The receiver loves this letter because they are getting a free gift, and they are appreciative of the endorser for providing it. And of course, you are happy because your Spa is being introduced to a new group of people who already value what you provide due to the personal endorsement you received.

The key in this method is to make the life of the endorser easy. Other than needing some of their letterhead and their database to send the letter out to, you should take care of everything else. You will write the letter (a sample is provided for you at the end of this section), you will address and stuff the envelopes, and you will mail them. Make sure that the gift you

Guerrilla Marketing for Spas

are giving away is of real value so the endorser can feel great knowing they are giving their clients something they will really appreciate (and so that the endorser would want to help you from the beginning – no one is going to sign up to help a Spa owner with something that only benefits the owner).

By writing the letter for the endorser, you are: 1) making it easy on them so that they will be more likely to help you out, 2) ensuring that the letter is completed and sent out quickly, and 3) making sure it is successful because you are writing copy that gets results. (We have provided an example of a well-written endorsement letter at the end of this section.) Be sure to personalize your letters in some way to the endorser and then allow them to approve the letter before you send them out. They are, after all, signing their name to it, so you need to make sure you are writing a letter they are comfortable with. Being careful to write the letter in their voice as they would write it will help with their level of comfort as well.

The letter needs to convey the results you provide for your clients. The readers want to know, "What is in it for me?" and that's really all they care about. Here is an example of an endorsement letter that delivers results:

Endorsement Letter Sample:

(On Endorser's letterhead)

Date

Client's name, title
Company name
Address

Dear Mr./Ms. Client,

I'm writing because I have something very important to tell you:

Thank you for your business.

Over the years you've been one of my most loyal clients. You've helped us grow to where we are today. So I wanted to do something unique to show you how much I truly appreciate having you as a client.

In the past year, I've received several treatments from a local Spa called (INSERT YOUR COMPANY NAME). As a token of my appreciation to you, I've arranged to have COMPANY NAME give you a comprehensive evaluation for (INSERT NAME OF YOUR EVALUATION).

Normally, COMPANY NAME charges a minimum of $150 for this service. But because I've purchased it for you, it's absolutely free. You see, I did come up with a very unique way to express my gratitude.

Now, COMPANY NAME isn't like other Spas you may have used. In fact, their clients swear that they have an uncanny ability to (INSERT YOUR SPECIALTY).

One of my friends, (INSERT NAME OF A CLIENT YOU ARE QUOTING) said this after a few sessions with COMPANY NAME:

"INSERT TESTIMONIAL."

Here's another example. One of COMPANY NAME's clients, (INSERT NAME OF CLIENT), who went to COMPANY NAME for (INSERT THE CLIENT'S ISSUE) said:

"INSERT TESTIMONIAL."

Another great example is from (INSERT NAME OF A FELLOW PROFESSIONAL WHO ENDORSES YOU), who reported:

"INSERT TESTIMONIAL."

I could go on, but I think you get the picture. And as I mentioned earlier, I've arranged for

COMPANY NAME to give you their unique services absolutely free.

By the way, your evaluation will be done with no strings attached and no obligation on your part.

Also, I'm not being compensated for this in any way. It's simply my way of expressing my appreciation for all the business you've given me over the years.

To be frank, I've never written this type of "thank you" letter before and I'm not really sure what to expect. COMPANY NAME will make every effort to get your assessment scheduled within 10 days of receiving your request. But if they are flooded with requests, please be patient.

To make sure your evaluation gets top priority, it would be best to return the enclosed form to COMPANY NAME as soon as possible.

Once again, I'd like to thank you for your continuing patronage.

Sincerely,

Your name
Your company

P.S. If you'd like to know more about COMPANY NAME, you can visit their website at: www.xyzHealthSpa.com. Be sure to take a look at their special report (INSERT *NAME OF YOUR FREE REPORT)* in the free newsletter section. It will show you how they (INSERT THE VALUE YOUR REPORT PROVIDES).

Then you want to include a certificate that accompanies the endorsed lead generation letter. Here is an example of that:

Certificate to Accompany Endorsement Letter Sample:

FREE

Energy and Wellness Evaluation

($150 Consultation Value)

This certificate entitles you to a free energy and wellness evaluation. Please send a brief description of your problem and any specific energy and wellness questions you have. COMPANY NAME will personally review and evaluate your information. You will receive a complete customized analysis at their office including strategies for quickly and safely restoring your energy and wellness.

(Please type or print clearly)

Name:

Title:

Company:

Address:

City, State, Zip:

Phone:

Fax:

E-mail:

Complete confidentiality guaranteed. Your appointment will be scheduled once we receive this form. Please allow 10 days for us to schedule your evaluation. This offer is available by mail only. Please complete both sides and send to:

YOUR NAME
YOUR COMPANY
YOUR ADDRESS

In order to help me make the most useful recommendations for your energy and wellness, please answer the following questions:

1. What kind of problem would you like resolved?

2. Do you have or have you had any energy and

wellness issues that might be keeping you from being the confident person you want to be (examples might include: low energy levels, complexion problems, trying to quit smoking, overweight and physically unfit, etc.)?

3. What are your three main energy and wellness goals?

1.

2.

3.

4. What health and fitness magazines and newsletters do you regularly read?

When choosing your endorsement partners, you are looking for service professionals, organizations, and associations whose clients are also your target market. For example, a gym doesn't offer the same services as you, but very likely might have a similar target market. Associations are the perfect organizations to endorse your services because they love to give added benefits to their members. Choose associations whose members would most likely be interested in the services you provide. It should also go without saying that in choosing an endorser, it needs to be someone you respect and trust. You are basically borrowing the credibility of the endorser in this approach, so it is imperative that the endorser has credibility himself.

Do a 2-minute drill brainstorming all of the different businesses and associations that could endorse you. Even consider your vendors.

It is important to compensate the endorser because it will help ensure they will allow this exchange to take place, and because Guerrilla marketers know that partnerships only exist when there is an equal exchange and when the best interests of both parties are at heart. You can compensate the endorser with an exchange of services or money. One of the best ways is to allow them to send an endorsement letter to your database as well. Another method is to take the free gift you are giving the endorser's list a step further and state that the endorser actually purchased your services for them. Endorsers like this option because it is a way that they can provide their clients with more value at no additional cost, but their clients will think it was an added cost and they will be appreciative of the endorser.

The way you approach potential endorsers is important because you want to make sure you are presenting the benefits to the endorser and their database, otherwise they could be quick to say no because they will think there is nothing in it for them.

Here is a sample letter to help you get those yeses:

Proposal Letter to Potential Endorsers Sample:

Date

Potential Endorser's name, title
Company name
Address

Dear (INSERT NAME),

I have a proposal that would be beneficial for both of our businesses.

I'd like to offer some of your better customers a free energy and wellness assessment.

Normally, I charge $150 to $250 for this service.

Here's how it would be beneficial to you. We would send your customers a letter telling them that you'd like to thank them for all of the business they've done with you.

As a token of your appreciation, you've "bought" them a $250 Spa energy and wellness evaluation.

Of course, I'm not actually going to charge you for the evaluations.

The first benefit is that your customers will greatly appreciate the gift. I never skimp on free evaluations. I give them the same attention I would a paying client.

Your customers will end up with a number of powerful suggestions for attaining their energy and wellness goals. This should increase their loyalty to your company and make them want to do even more business with you.

The second benefit is that if they implement my suggestions, their energy and wellness will definitely improve. Then, they can continue to look and feel younger and more energetic each day.

The evaluation will be done with no strings attached and no obligation on your customers' part.

The benefit to me is that at some point, they may hire me for their Spa needs.

To make things as simple as possible for you, I will write the letter that you'll send to your customers (plus, I'll pay for the printing and postage). Of course, you'll have complete approval of every word that's in the letter.

That's the proposal. I hope you'll agree that this could be very beneficial for both of us. I'll give you a call in a few days to see if you're interested in this.

Sincerely,

YOUR NAME
YOUR COMPANY

Testimonials

Another way to gain credibility is to collect testimonials from happy clients. Collecting testimonials is something Guerrilla marketers do on a regular basis. They ask for the testimonial right at the point when the client has expressed how excited they are with the results they received from the service. Ask them to jot it down for you or ask if you can video record them doing a quick testimonial. These days, this is easier than ever with cell phones that double as a recording device.

For clients who aren't comfortable with writing or recording a testimonial for you, ask if you can write one for them and sign their name to it. You have heard them rave about your services so you can paraphrase what they said adding in even more about

Guerrilla Marketing for Spas

what you want people to know about you if you'd like. Then just be sure to send it to the client for their approval before signing their name to it.

Another way to approach testimonials is similar to the endorsement letter. You can search for other service professionals who know you and the services you provide, and ask if they would sign their name to a testimonial you have written for them.

In using your testimonials, don't be stingy. Guerrilla marketers use testimonials on almost every marketing platform because they understand their power. If a person looked at two Spa websites, both of which talked about their services, but only one had testimonials throughout the site, which Spa do you think that person would be more inclined to call – the one that others are raving about, or the one that is only raving about itself?

Guerrilla Marketing for Spas

Testimonials seal the deal. If a person is on the fence and there are testimonials from other happy clients, they are much more likely to turn that indecision into decision. For that reason, don't be afraid to interject them into all of your marketing approaches. You can add them on the back of your business card, add them to your brochure, and include them on postcards and on direct mail letters. They can be placed in ads, in articles and in blog posts. On your website, it is common to have a separate testimonials page, but Guerrilla marketers also sprinkle them throughout the other pages on their site. Websites are also great places for adding video testimonials, which are even more effective.

At times, you can use a testimonial request letter to collect testimonials. Here is a template to work from:

Testimonial Request Letter Sample:

Date

Client's name, title
Address

Dear CLIENT'S NAME,

Thank you for the opportunity to assist you in (INSERT THE PROBLEM YOU HELPED THEM SOLVE). I'm pleased to hear that the early results have been exceptional.

I know you're extremely busy, but if you'd be so kind, I'd like to ask a favor of you.

I'm in the process of putting together a list of testimonials – a collection of comments about my services from clients like you.

Would you take a few minutes to give me your opinion of how my services contributed to (INSERT THE PROBLEM YOUR SERVICES FIXED

FOR THEM)? No need to dictate a letter – just jot your comments on the back of this letter, sign below, and return to me in the enclosed envelope.

If you'll be kind enough to give me your comments, I'll be happy to return the favor by sending you a complimentary copy of my CD: **(INSERT NAME OF YOUR CD)**. I'm sure you'll find it very useful for restoring your energy and accomplishing your wellness goals.

I look forward to learning what you liked about my services... but I also welcome any suggestions or criticisms, too.

Many thanks, (INSERT NAME OF CLIENT).

Regards,

YOUR NAME

You have my permission to quote from my comments, and use these quotations in ads and promotions used to market your products and services.

Signature:

Date:

Case Studies

Another radically effective form of marketing that is often left out of marketing plans is the use of case studies. It is easy to do once you have started collecting testimonials because you just turn those testimonials into case studies. It is as simple as describing the problem the client had when they came to see you, then describing the treatment plan you created for the client, and explaining the results they received and how it has impacted their lives.

Case studies can be used in so many ways, and since Guerrilla marketers always leverage their marketing efforts, you should be sure to use them in at least three different ways. First, print them out and bind them in a book that you can keep in your lobby for clients to look over. They can also be used as articles in magazines, on your website, as a blog post, in your newsletter or e-zine, on your Facebook page, sent out as direct mail letters, and sent to newspapers (they love human interest stories like these).

When using case studies as articles, be sure to include something free that the readers can download from your website like a free report or an e-book, or give them a way to sign up for a free evaluation. Again, you are doing people a disservice by providing them information but then not giving them a way to get help. By offering something for free, you are giving them the opportunity to have their issue resolved, and that is what you should explain to a publication that gives you a hard time about including your free offering.

Case studies can also be turned into client success articles, which are extremely effective and are also easy to get printed as human interest stories for free publicity.

Here is an example written for a Spa that you can use to guide you in writing your client success article:

Client Success Article Sample:

(NAME OF YOUR SPA)'s Client Reporter

DATE

Copyright YEAR by YOUR FULL NAME

How A Client Went From Fried Hair to Luxurious Health and Shine In One Treatment – And How You Can Do The Same

by YOUR FULL NAME

The amount of confidence a woman has often, unfortunately, comes from her appearance, especially from her hair. Hair color and highlights become a normal part of most women's regimen as the gray sets in. If it isn't done right, overworked hair can lash out and become dry, brittle and downright fried.

The fact is that in this day and age, women don't need to live with fried hair. With new gentle hair treatments and highly skilled practitioners, healthy, shiny, soft hair is possible.

How A Women Went From Fried to Luxurious in ONE Treatment.

Betty Jones had been getting her fine, curly, long hair colored for over 20 years, and her hair stylist had been putting the color on for too long. The outcome was hair that was extremely dry and breaking off.

Fortunately, all of that turned around when Betty was given a gift certificate to XYZ Health Spa, along with a recommendation that they were the best Spa for hair treatments in miles around. She came in a nervous wreck, worried her hair would be damaged even more by yet another treatment. The results she got, however, eased her stress within seconds as she realized that her hair was restored to the soft, shiny, youthful hair she once knew.

Betty's hair was treated with gentle and natural emollients that helped to moisturize and heal her hair strands. The result? Thicker and healthier looking hair.

She reported to XYZ Health Spa that she was extremely impressed with how comfortable she was made to feel throughout the whole process.

Guerrilla Marketing for Spas

She thanked them for how much they listened and were able to create results beyond what she imagined.

If you suffer from dry, brittle, damaged and overworked hair, you really can get back to the hair you used to have. You'll find that youthful confidence is waiting for you and it can happen fast.

Fusion Marketing

The ultimate way to market like a Guerrilla is with fusion marketing, also known as joint venturing. Endorsement letters, as explained earlier, are a form of fusion marketing, but there are numerous additional ways to fusion market as well. Guerrilla marketers use creativity to come up with new ways to partner with others that will benefit both parties. Some additional ideas will be presented here, but always keep creativity flowing in your own mind, because the possibilities are truly endless.

Fusion marketing is nothing more than coming up with a way to work together with another professional to cross-promote your products and services. The results are always a win-win for both parties involved.

You already did a 2-minute drill in the endorsement letter section to determine who would be good people to partner with. You might want to do another 2-minute drill to add to that list. Since fusion marketing offers unlimited possibilities in how you can partner with someone, you might come to think of more people than you thought of for the endorsement letter exercise. Who has the same type of clientele as you? Who has a large following of the people who fall into your target market? Who do you respect and value? Who could benefit from partnering with you?

Now do another 2-minute drill to come up with fusion marketing ideas. Again, be sure not to limit yourself. Write down anything and everything you can think of. Here are some examples to help you get started:

You might know that women who frequent beauty salons fall into your target market. What salons in your area could you approach? What ways can you create a win-win between your Spa and the salon? Perhaps you could each hand out gift certificates as a gift to your clientele. If they have a large database and you don't, you could ask them to promote your Spa in their e-zine and in return you would give them a percentage of the sales generated. You could also consider creating a package together offering a combination of salon and Spa services. What else can you think of?

Get creative. Get in the Guerrilla mindset. There are so many ways to exchange value between two companies. It could be that a seminar is being offered and you know the people attending are also people who would be interested in your services. Ask the speaker if you can help out the day of the event and if you can provide him/her with gift certificates for a free evaluation that can be handed out in the attendees' take-home bags. This gives the speaker an additional gift to hand out so it is also welcomed.

Affiliate marketing is a popular form of fusion marketing. As an affiliate, you can sell other people's products and services on your website or in whatever manner you'd like, and since you are given a unique URL, any sales you generate are automatically tracked and you receive a commission. You could easily find some products and services that complement what you do and offer them in this way. You might also want to create your own affiliate program that would allow others to offer your services, packages, and products to generate commission for them. This is like having your own sales force available to you and you don't need to pay them unless they make sales.

Fusion marketing is one of the easiest and quickest ways to grow. Guerrilla marketers *always* have their fusion marketing radar on. Whenever they meet someone new, their creative minds start churning with ideas. They create alliances wherever they go. They don't practice competitiveness; they practice cooperation. The real key to fusion marketing is thinking of the other person first. Who can you help? What do you have to offer others? People want

Guerrilla Marketing for Spas

to work in partnership with people who provide value for them instead of thinking constantly of themselves. The next time you meet someone who might be a potential alliance, ask him or her, "How can I help you in your business?" When you approach your partnerships from that perspective, you will create an army of alliances who are willing and ready to help you succeed.

Guerrilla Marketing for Spas

Chapter 6 - Be the Expert

Guerrilla marketers set themselves up as experts, because they know that people like to buy from experts. Let's look at a case in which two Spas are in a 10-mile radius of one another. Spa A is known in the area for providing valuable information to the community, and Spa B is not. Which one do you think will gain more business? Most likely, it will be Spa A. This is because people learn to trust them and view them as experts in their field. That is not to say that Spa B doesn't have the same level of expertise, but without others gaining the perception that they are experts, Spa A will continue to be more popular.

Anyone can present themselves as an expert, and in this Information Age, doing so is almost required if you are to be successful. There are several ways to go about it, such as getting published, holding seminars, teleseminars or webinars, and offering information in the form of free give-aways. We'll discuss these in more detail now.

Get Published

If you are a Guerrilla marketer, you want to get published in one form or another because you know it will give you much needed exposure. When you see an article by a healthcare professional or an interview about them, don't you generally gain more respect for them? Don't you feel that person is an expert? Don't you trust what they say more than a healthcare professional that doesn't appear in print? Of course. It's just human nature to feel that people who are published are experts.

Guerrilla Marketing for Spas

Knowing that, it is important to find a way to get published so you can build up your credibility and expert-status. Don't shy away from the word "published." All it means is for your words to be put in print in one way or another. It could be through a book you wrote, an article you wrote that gets printed in a newspaper or magazine, or an interview conducted by a trade paper. But it could also be as simple as writing your own short e-book, or writing an article and offering it on your website or on a colleague's website, or creating a blog and posting valuable, consistent content. Don't overcomplicate it. Start with what is easy for you and get published now.

If you are a writer and you enjoy putting your knowledge into written words, you might want to use another Guerrilla weapon, which is to not only write articles, but to land a column in a newspaper or magazine, or be a monthly contributing author to a magazine. This will give you exceptional expert status, but getting there means you will need to start with some individual articles and a means of publication first.

For those of you who quiver at the idea of writing, there are many options available to you. You can use a ghostwriter, which is a person who writes for you in your name. There are also numerous article sites that allow you to inexpensively purchase articles and sign your name to them. Some examples of such sites include: www.articlecircle.com, www.articlesfactory.com, www.articlecity.com and www.freearticles.com. You can also ask someone to interview you, and then put that in print as well.

In a 2-minute drill, come up with how you can get yourself published quickly. What ways resonate with you the most? What would you like to start with? What would you like to aspire to?

Seminars, Tele-seminars, Webinars

Another way to present yourself as an expert is to offer seminars, teleseminars or webinars on a topic related to your services. Some people have no problem standing in front of a group of people speaking about a subject they are passionate about. For others, though, that can seem out of the question. In those cases, teleseminars and webinars make it easier since you are just talking through a phone or computer. In that situation, it is easy to read from notes and feel more comfortable speaking. Plus, it provides people with information they can get in the comfort of their own home. No matter which way you choose, speaking in any of these ways certainly will turn you into an expert.

You may choose to offer your seminar at no charge, which will probably get you the most attendees. Or you could offer it at a small cost, which would most likely get you fewer attendees, but those attendees tend to be more serious and therefore more interested in purchasing services. Both strategies are effective depending on what you are trying to do.

Do a 2-minute drill to come up with topics you could teach. What service are you most passionate about? What do clients rave about the most after you have treated them? What are the most common questions you get that you know people would like answered?

Guerrilla Marketing for Spas

Now use some of the Guerrilla marketing strategies you have learned to get the word out about your class.

Free Give-Aways

There is a saying, "There is nothing free in this world," but that saying went out when the Internet came in. Information is something that people can create once, and then re-use it over and over again. That is one of the reasons why information is the number one thing that is given out for free nowadays.

Guerrilla marketers know that if you want to succeed in the Information Age, you need to participate in the Information Age. With the Internet at the seat of communication these days, information is being handed out freely in droves. When people go online they want information and they want it to be free. Many people nowadays will not buy from someone until they have received some free information from that person. It makes sense because they need to be able to trust the person they are buying from, and getting information from them gives them that trust.

If you are not giving your clients and potential clients free information, you are leaving them in the dark about what you really do; therefore why should they trust you? They need a taste of you and what you offer so they can make an informed decision about whether to hire you or not. Wouldn't you want the same?

A free give-away serves to not only present you as an expert, but it also is a means for you to increase your database. By having an opt-in form on your website where someone can sign up to receive your free e-book, for example, you now have access to their name and e-mail address so that you can add them to your keep-in-touch program. Be sure to never spam them though. You should always have an unsubscribe link where they can opt-out of your list should they choose to. The great thing about an opt-in form is that it creates a permission-based list – one where the people on the list asked to be on the list by showing an interest in what you are offering. That is powerful because it gives you a list of definitely interested potential clients.

Again, as a Guerrilla, think creatively about what you can offer as a free give-away. Giving away information certainly tends to be the least expensive give-away since there are usually no out-of-pocket costs for you. As PDF's, you could give away an e-book, a special report, a book of articles, a book of your case studies, a tip sheet, a checklist, a list of myths or a fitness guide. You could give away an mp3 recording of one of your teleseminars or a video or one of your seminars. You can also give away things like gift certificates for a free evaluation.

Do a 2-minute drill to come up with all the ideas you can think of for free give-aways that you could easily put together and that your target audience would want to have.

Chapter 7 - Leveraging Your Marketing Efforts

Ideas for Gaining Leverage

You've actually already been introduced to many leveraging strategies in this book thus far, but it is important to spend some time gaining a true understanding of the concept of leveraging so you can think like a Guerrilla. Since marketing needs to be consistent and since you need to launch many weapons at once, you need to have a way to make that process a little easier and less labor intensive so you can actually accomplish it. Leveraging is what will do that for you.

Guerrillas always work smart. They know that the work they put into one marketing strategy can often be carried over into several other strategies, and they make full use of that fact.

Anytime you create a new marketing strategy, ask yourself in the beginning stages of planning how you can leverage that strategy. For example, if you plan to get published to increase your expert status and you decide to write an article that you can e-mail to your list, immediately come up with at least three additional ways you can use that article. Can you mail it to prospective clients? Can you ask colleagues to print it in their newsletter? Can you print some out and put them in your lobby as take-aways? Can you add it to your website?

In another example, let's say you are going to hold a teleseminar, and in order to leverage that effort, you decide to record the class so you can use it for a number of additional marketing weapons, such

Guerrilla Marketing for Spas

as using it for a free give-away, sending it to existing clients as a free gift, or making a CD series out of all of your teleseminars to sell.

If a marketing tactic you are developing is to create a case studies book to display in your lobby, you might also consider using those case studies as articles in your e-zine, mailing one at a time to prospective clients over a period of time, sending the one that pertains to the prospect the most to them after conducting a free evaluation for them, posting them on your website, sending them with press releases to publications, or attaching them with your endorsement or direct mail letters.

Always remember to leverage every marketing strategy you undergo. Otherwise you will end up running yourself ragged. Marketing can be time consuming, so be sure you are working smart.

Guerrilla Marketing for Spas

Leveraging also serves to create a consistent message among numerous marketing strategies, and it allows you to get in front of people from many different angles.

Terri's Big Leverage Technique

If you want to grow *fast*, this is the method to use. You'll want to contact other professionals that your ideal clients are already doing business with and have them sponsor you by giving away your information products (such as a CD or booklet) for free to those clients. You could even offer your information products to be given out in goodie bags at speaking events where the audience happens to be your target market.

This allows the professional to provide additional value to their clients, and it allows you to get in front of your ideal target market in a way that is non-sales-like. This technique is extremely powerful because by having your information products given out as a gift from a trusted professional, the ideal clients are more open to reviewing the product and then contacting you after they like what they hear or see.

Another way to use this technique is to contact the associations and organizations whose members are your ideal clients as well, and offer them your information products to give away as an added bonus to their members. Associations love to give more value to their members, especially when it doesn't cost them anything, so offering your products is something they are usually happy to take part in.

Guerrilla Marketing for Spas

By using this strategy, you have just leveraged your information products as well as your time and energy, because you are getting in front of the right people in a super effective manner. This method also allows you to leverage the credibility of another professional, causing you to become a trusted professional in the eyes of potential ideal clients just because they already trust the person who gave them your product. All of this leveraging at once is what makes this *Terri's Big Leverage Technique*. It's not often you can leverage so much in one shot.

Here is a sample letter you can use to create professional alliances such as these:

Fusion Marketing Letter Sample:

Date

Name, title

Company name
Address

Dear NAME,

I have a bonus item to offer you to give to your seminar attendees. I've just completed a new CD called, "How to Renew Your Youthful Energy." I've enclosed a copy of the CD for your review.

As you'll see, this CD details a very simple, yet extremely powerful way to make simple steps in one's daily life that can help restore your energy levels and make you feel 10 years younger. And it requires no additional expense whatsoever.

Clients I've introduced this technique to rave about the results they've produced.

I'd be happy to give all of your seminar attendees a copy of this CD and I'll make the terms very attractive for you.

I can provide you with as many copies of the CD as you'd like for just $1.00 per CD, labeled and enclosed in a plastic case.

Since this CD normally sells for $27, you can promote it as having that value to your attendees.

If you're interested in adding extra value for your attendees, just let me know how many copies you'd like and I'll have my duplication house get rolling. It takes roughly ten days from the time I notify my vendor until I have the CD's in hand.

Thanks. I'll look forward to hearing back from you soon.

Warm regards,

YOUR NAME
YOUR COMPANY

Chapter 8 - Planning Your Attack

Now that you have taken a look at some of the most effective marketing weapons for Spa owners, you can begin to map out your plan of action. Successful marketing happens by having the end in sight. It begins by being aware of all the marketing strategies that are available, launching the ones you feel will create the best results, and then tracking which ones are hitting the target and which ones are not. As time goes on, the successful marketer eliminates the weapons that miss the target and doubles up on those that hit it.

In order to properly manage and track your marketing weapons, it is necessary to be organized and to follow a timeline. That timeline is organized and maintained best when it is tracked on a *marketing calendar*.

Without having a marketing calendar, your marketing will be hit-or-miss and you will have lapses in time where your marketing efforts fall by the wayside. Using a marketing calendar is thought by most Guerrilla marketers to be their most precious asset. It will allow you to clearly outline all of your weapons and to make sure they work together. It will enable you to plan your budget and avoid unforeseen expenditures.

The goal of the marketing calendar is to create results, which can only be won through intentionality, accountability, and consistency, all of which lead to profits.

Guerrilla Marketing for Spas

To begin, Guerrilla marketers always start with the end, planning backwards from the attainment of their goals, to the present. They do this because the path to success is illuminated when working in this way. The Spas that work only from the beginning without seeing where they want to end up are shortsighted, and therefore, they are caught off guard when unforeseen circumstances arise. When you start from the end instead and your path is illuminated as a result, you will already have planned for those circumstances, and any that are still left unforeseen will not hinder you as much as they would without having a plan in place.

The hardest part of planning your marketing is being able to see the target. It is necessary to act like you already have the end result you want, because it is only by seeing what must be accomplished in order

Guerrilla Marketing for Spas

to have the success you seek that you can recognize where you need to be and how you need to be acting at each point along the way. It leads you to a backwards plan of action that ends at your target.

The marketing calendar of a Guerrilla is one that accounts for change and flexibility, and it's one that factors in success and growth. It leaves room for expansion and diversification. It gives the business a plan to operate in the here and now, while also holding a sharp focus on the there and then.

Creating Your Marketing Calendar

To create your Guerrilla marketing calendar, start with a number of rows and 5 columns. The first column is called "Weapon," referring to which marketing weapon you'll use. The second column is called "Cost." That is where you will project how much you will spend on that marketing weapon. The third column is called "Comments," and this is where you add any details that need to be explained about the marketing method you are using. The fourth column is called "Date." This is where you list what date you will complete that marketing weapon by. The fifth and final column is called "Results," and this is where you provide a letter grade to the marketing effort (A, B, C, D or F). This allows you to easily see which weapons are hitting the target and which ones are not.

At the end of the year, the Guerrilla marketer will look back over the year by comparing his sales figures with his marketing calendar. He'll eliminate all of the weapons that were not graded with an A or B. By the third year of persisting with this process, the Guerrilla marketer will start to see a calendar that is

Guerrilla Marketing for Spas

loaded with slam-dunks, and their Spa will be buzzing with clients. For those who don't follow this type of system and haphazardly handle their marketing, they will continue to stumble from marketing method to marketing method without getting lasting results. To get yourself in the zone of success, create your marketing calendar today. Here is an example to help you:

Weapon	Cost	Comments	Date	Results
1. E-zine	$0	Goal to increase readership to 1000 monthly	12/1	
2. Follow-up	$0	Make list of 5 prospects or former clients and contact them	Everyday	
3. Trade Links	$0	Contact 3 fusion marketing partners to propose trading links	11/15	
4. Classified Ad	$50	Place 1 classified ad in the Inquirer	11/27	

Guerrilla Marketing for Spas

5. New services announcement letter	$100	Write and send letter to all people on mailing list	11/25
6. Book 2 lectures	$0	Call 2 associations to book seminars	11/7
7. Gain 2 Endorsement partners	$200	Send endorsement letters to their databases	12/10
8. Hire copywriter for website	$400	Rewrite website for better marketing results	12/15
9. Add opt-in form to website	$75	Add form to website where people can download my free report	12/15
10. Write free report	$0	Write the report they will download from the opt-in form	12/14

Conclusion

Hopefully by now, it is evident to you that the small business owner can succeed in the world of marketing these days. It doesn't require a ton of money and it doesn't require a degree in marketing. As you know, what it does require is creativity of thought and an investment of time and energy. The ideas in this book can serve as your arsenal of weapons that will set you up for success.

The true essence of a Guerrilla marketer is a creative spirit. Don't limit yourself. Keep your creative juices flowing at all times. Always be open to new ideas that might come to you. There is an unending supply of effective Guerrilla marketing tactics out there, many of which have yet to be discovered.

Guerrilla Marketing for Spas

If you've made it through this book without doing the activities and the 2-minute drills, now is the time to go back and begin. To be an effective marketer and to have a Spa that is overflowing with clients, you will need to have discipline when it comes to your marketing plan. Set yourself up for success starting now. Become a Guerrilla and market your way to success.

Guerrilla Marketing for Spas

The 200 Weapons of Guerrilla Marketing

Minimedia

1. Marketing Plan
2. Marketing Calendar
3. Identity
4. Business Cards
5. Stationery
6. Personal Letters
7. Telephone Marketing
8. Toll-Free Number
9. Vanity Phone Number
10. Yellow Pages
11. Postcards
12. Postcard Deck
13. Classified Ads
14. Per Order/Inquiry Advertising
15. Free Ads in Shoppers
16. Circulars
17. Community Bulletin Boards
18. Movie Ads
19. Outside Signs
20. Street Banners
21. Window Display
22. Inside Signs
23. Posters
24. Canvassing
25. Door Hangers
26. Elevator Pitch
27. Value Story
28. Back-End Sales

Guerrilla Marketing for Spas

29. Letters of Recommendation
30. Attendance at Trade Shows

Maximedia

31. Advertising
32. Direct Mail
33. Newspaper Ads
34. Radio Spots
35. Magazine Ads
36. Billboards
37. Television Commercials

E-Media

38. Computer
39. Printer/Fax
40. Chat Rooms
41. Forums Boards
42. Internet Bulletin Boards
43. List Building
44. Personalized E-mail
45. E-mail Signature
46. Canned E-mail
47. Bulk E-mail
48. Audio/Video Postcards
49. Domain Name
50. Website
51. Landing Page
52. Merchant Account
53. Shopping Cart
54. Autoresponders
55. Search Engine Ranking
56. Electronic Brochures
57. RSS Feeds

Guerrilla Marketing for Spas

58. Blogs
59. Podcasting
60. Own E-Zine
61. Ads in Other E-Zines
62. E-Books
63. Content for Other Sites
64. Webinars
65. Joint Ventures
66. Word of Mouse
67. Viral Marketing
68. EBay/Auction Sites
69. Click Analyzers
70. Pay Per Click Ads
71. Search Engine Keywords
72. Google Adwords
73. Sponsored Links
74. Reciprocal Link Exchanges
75. Banner Exchanges
76. Web Conversion Rate

Info-Media

77. Knowledge of Your Market
78. Research Studies
79. Specific Customer Data
80. Case Studies
81. Sharing
82. Brochures
83. Catalog
84. Business Directory
85. Public Service Announcements
86. Newsletter
87. Speech
88. Free Consultations

Guerrilla Marketing for Spas

89. Free Demonstrations
90. Free Seminars
91. Article
92. Column
93. Book
94. Publishing on Demand
95. Speaker at Clubs
96. Teleseminars
97. Infomercials
98. Constant Learning

Human Media

99. Marketing Insight
100. Yourself
101. Your Employees and Reps
102. Designated Guerrilla
103. Employee Attire
104. Social Demeanor
105. Target Audiences
106. Your Own Circle of Influence
107. Contact Time With Customers
108. How You Say Hello and Good-Bye
109. Teaching Ability
110. Stories
111. Sales Training
112. Use of Downtime
113. Networking
114. Professional Title
115. Affiliate Marketing
116. Media Contacts
117. A-list Customers
118. Core Story
119. Sense of Urgency

120. Offer Limited Items/Time
121. Call-to-Action
122. Satisfied Customers

Non-media

123. Benefits List
124. Competitive Advantages
125. Gifts
126. Service
127. Public Relations
128. Fusion Marketing
129. Barter
130. Word of Mouth
131. Buzz
132. Community Involvement
133. Club and Association Memberships
134. Free Directory Listings
135. Trade Show Booth
136. Special Events
137. Name Tags at Events
138. Luxury Box at Events
139. Gift Certificates
140. Audiovisual Aids
141. Flipcharts
142. Reprints and Blowups
143. Coupons
144. Free-Trial Offer
145. Guarantee
146. Contests and Sweepstakes
147. Baking or Craft Ability
148. Lead Buying
149. Follow-up
150. Tracking Plan

Guerrilla Marketing for Spas

151. Marketing On Hold
152. Branded Entertainment
153. Product Placement
154. Radio Talk Show Guest
155. TV Talk Show Guest
156. Subliminal Marketing

Company Attributes

157. Proper View of Marketing
158. Brand Name Awareness
159. Positioning
160. Name
161. Meme
162. Theme Line
163. Writing Ability
164. Copywriting Ability
165. Headline Copy
166. Location
167. Hours of Operation
168. Days of Operation
169. Credit Cards Accepted
170. Financing Available
171. Credibility
172. Reputation
173. Efficiency
174. Quality
175. Service
176. Selection
177. Price
178. Opportunities to Upgrade
179. Referral Program
180. Spying
181. Testimonials

Guerrilla Marketing for Spas

182. Extra Value
183. Noble Cause

Company Attributes

184. Easy To Do Business With
185. Honest Interest in People
186. Telephone Demeanor
187. Passion and Enthusiasm
188. Sensitivity
189. Patience
190. Flexibility
191. Generosity
192. Self-Confidence
193. Neatness
194. Aggressiveness
195. Competitiveness
196. High Energy
197. Speed
198. Focus
199. Attention to Details
200. Action

Made in the USA
Coppell, TX
14 June 2024